At David C Cook, we equip the local church around the corner and around the globe to make disciples. Come see how we are working together—go to **www.davidccook.com**. Thank you!

KNOWING GOD THE FATHER

DAVID C COOK FAMILY DEVOTIONS

KNOWING GOD THE FATHER

52 Devotions to Grow Your Family's Faith

DAVID **C** COOK

transforming lives together

KNOWING GOD THE FATHER
Published by David C Cook
4050 Lee Vance Drive
Colorado Springs, CO 80918 U.S.A.

Integrity Music Limited, a Division of David C Cook
Eastbourne, East Sussex BN23 6NT, England

The graphic circle C logo is a registered trademark of David C Cook.

All rights reserved. Except for brief excerpts for review purposes,
no part of this book may be reproduced or used in any form
without written permission from the publisher.

Unless otherwise indicated, all Scripture quotations are taken from
THE HOLY BIBLE, NEW INTERNATIONAL VERSION®,
NIV® Copyright © 1973, 1978, 1984, 2011 by Biblica, Inc.® Used
by permission. All rights reserved worldwide. Scripture quotations
marked CEV are taken from the Contemporary English Version ©
1991, 1995 by American Bible Society. Used by permission; NCV are
taken from the New Century Version®. Copyright © 2005 by Thomas
Nelson. Used by permission. All rights reserved; NLT are taken from
the *Holy Bible*, New Living Translation, copyright © 1996, 2007 by
Tyndale House Foundation. Used by permission of Tyndale House
Publishers, Inc., Carol Stream, Illinois 60188. All rights reserved.

LCCN 2017964361
ISBN 978-1-4347-1249-3
eISBN 978-0-8307-7575-0

© 2018 Beers Family Real Estate LLC
Published in association with the literary agency of
Mark Sweeney & Associates, Naples, FL 34113.

The Team: Lindsay Black, Jeff Gerke, Rachael Stevenson, Jane Ann Kenney
Cover Design: Nick Lee
Cover Illustration: Oliver Genoux

Printed in the United States of America
First Edition 2018

1 2 3 4 5 6 7 8 9 10

062818

CONTENTS

NOTE TO PARENTS

You are about to begin a delightful journey with a child, using this book as your road map. Whether you are a parent, grandparent, uncle, aunt, teacher, neighbor, or some other special person with the great privilege of leading children God's way, praise God for you.

This is a devotional book to help children—*and* you—know God the Father better, love Him more deeply, and serve Him more effectively.

The first section in every devotion is a poetry-style passage to read aloud to your child. This is designed to engage your child with the opening Bible verse in a way that lights their imagination and touches their hearts.

The "Grow Your Faith" section is for you to read to yourself, perhaps before you sit down with your child. This section leads you to interact with the passage and some aspect of God the Father in a way that may challenge and inspire you. This could help prepare you if the other parts of the reading give rise to a discussion with your child.

This is followed by a section called "Grow Your Child's Faith." This is also designed to be read aloud to your child. It extends the original thought and brings application in ways he or she can use in real life.

Each devotion concludes with a suggested prayer your child could say to God the Father. If a prayer isn't exactly what your child is thinking or feeling right then, encourage him or her to adjust it so it becomes an authentic expression to God.

It is our prayer that as you and your child learn more about God the Father, you will forge an unforgettable bond in which your hearts and God's heart become knitted together in love.

GOD IS OUR HEAVENLY FATHER

"Our Father in heaven ..."
Matthew 6:9

What would the perfect father be like?

The perfect father is strong
but so, so loving.
The perfect father is brave
and keeps little ones safe.

Laughter in the morning.
Kisses at night.
"I'm so proud of you, my child.
I'll always be here for you."

Whatever the perfect father is,
that's what *God* the Father is ...
times a billion.

Grow Your Faith

What's your favorite characteristic of the perfect father? Whether you're a man or woman, this child's father or not, find a way to demonstrate that characteristic to this child today. May you learn something about your heavenly Father as a result.

Grow Your Child's Faith

What's your favorite thing about any father you've ever known, seen, or just heard about? God is even better than that all the time. He would fight any enemy and cross any distance to keep you safe all the way to the end.

Dear Father, thank You that all the most perfect things a father could ever be are all the things You always are! Amen.

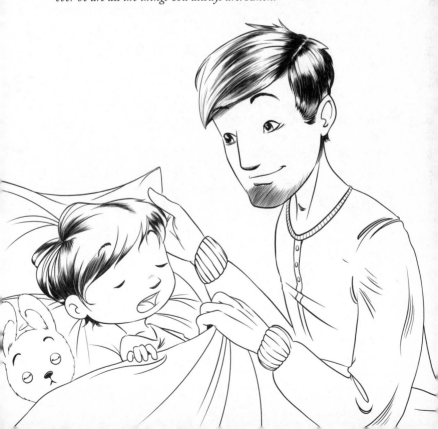

GOD THE FATHER HAS HOLY NAMES

"May your name always be kept holy."
Matthew 6:9 NCV

What if you didn't have a name?
What would you call yourself?
Who would you be?

What if *God* didn't have a name?

When Jesus told people how to pray,
He said, "Our Father in heaven, Your name is holy."
Holy means "pure" and "perfect,"
but it also means "different."

Take one minute with your eyes closed
and think of God as holy.

Grow Your Faith

Find a list online of the names of God and speak each one with a hush. Stand before Him in silence and gratitude, knowing that I AM has said "I love you" to you.

Grow Your Child's Faith

God wants us to say His name. But He doesn't want us to be thoughtless when we use His name, because He really *is* holy and pure. You are special to God, and He knows your name too!

Dear Father, thank You that I can call You Daddy. I'm so glad You know my name and know it's me when I pray. Amen.

3

GOD'S WILL SHOULD BE DONE

"May your will be done on earth, as it is in heaven."
Matthew 6:10 NLT

Do you ever want something
you can't have?

Did you know that even God
doesn't get everything He wants?

He wants everyone to love Him,
but not everyone does.

God loves to be in any and every place.
What if your heart was one of those places?

Grow Your Faith

What about you? Is your heart one of the places where God's will is done on earth as it is in heaven? Identify an area today where you have kept the door locked against Him … and invite Him in.

Grow Your Child's Faith

What's one thing God would like for you to do? Maybe you know someone who gets left out at recess. Maybe you could go be his or her friend. If you do, it will make God smile.

Dear Father, I really want my heart to be one of the places where You get everything You want. Will You please do that in me? Amen.

GOD IS THE CREATOR

In the beginning God created the heavens and the earth.
Genesis 1:1

Once upon a time,
only one being existed:
God.

Then He spoke,
and the universe was born.

Grow Your Faith

Though we may feel big and important, you and I make up an infinitely small portion of the universe. We're actually extremely small. And yet, God the Father holds us in such high esteem that the universe is tiny in comparison to His love for you and me.

Grow Your Child's Faith

God had an idea of what the whole universe could be like. And then He made it. Today or tomorrow, make something from an idea in your mind … and in that way, you are being a creator too.

Dear Father, You're so amazing to have created everything from nothing. Thank You for making me. Amen.

GOD GIVES US AN EVERLASTING PROMISE

*"When I see the rainbow in the sky, I will always remember
the promise that I have made to every living creature."*
Genesis 9:16 CEV

Once, long ago, people made God so sad
He had even made them
that He sent a flood
to wipe the earth clean.

When the few survivors—
people and animals—
stepped out of the ark onto dry land,
they saw something new in the sky.

A rainbow!

God said the rainbow sealed His promise
that He would never flood the earth again.
God keeps His promises.

Grow Your Faith

If there's one thing you can count on about God, it's that He remains forever true to His promises, His people, and His character. A rainbow, that delightful refraction and dispersion of light, is a reminder that God keeps His promises. What's a promise you haven't kept? What step could you take to remedy the situation? God is all about fresh starts.

Grow Your Child's Faith

Have you ever broken a promise? Have you had the chance to go make it right? God always keeps His promises, and we can be like Him and keep ours.

Dear Father, thank You for always keeping Your promises! I'm sorry I don't always keep mine. Please help me be more like You! Amen.

GOD'S PRESENCE IS HOLINESS

"The place where you are standing is holy ground."
Exodus 3:5

Wherever God is,
is holy.
And God is everywhere
all at the same time.

When you read about God,
He's there.
When you talk to God,
He's there.

This place here, right now,
is a place where God is.
This is a special moment with God,
and anything could happen.

Grow Your Faith

Human beings can experience God's holiness—how special and perfect He is—when He is present. When do you sense the presence of God's holiness?

Grow Your Child's Faith

There are so many things about God that are special. In fact, when we say God is holy, we are really saying that He is special. God is holy, and God makes everywhere He is holy too. When He lives in you, you are holy too.

Dear Father, thank You that wherever You are, that place is special— because I know You're here with me! Amen.

GOD IS WITH US

God said, "I will be with you."
Exodus 3:12

Sometimes, I like to be alone
to do what I want.
There are other times when I really *don't*
want to be alone.

Sometimes, I need someone to hold my hand
or take me into a big hug.

Did you know God the Father is *your* Father?
Did you know He will hold your hand and hug you forever?

Grow Your Faith

It's one of those not-very-well-kept secrets that adults get scared a lot. We never outgrow the need to have someone bigger and stronger come hold our hand. And that's okay. Maybe that's even the whole idea.

Grow Your Child's Faith

There once was a little girl who got lost at a park. She was scared, but she called her daddy and followed his voice until they saw each other in person and he could take her into his arms. That's what it's like to be a Christian. When we pray, it's like talking to God.

He's watching and listening to us all the time, even when we aren't calling Him. And one day, we'll see Him in person.

Dear Father, thank You for always hearing me when I call for You. Thank You for always taking time for me. Amen.

GOD GIVES US EVERY BREATH

"God … gives breath to all living things."
Numbers 16:22

To bring Adam to life,
God put breath into him.
To be alive is to take breaths.

One day, we'll breathe our last breath.
We'll go to God the Father …
and breathe the air of heaven.

Grow Your Faith

Only God can give breath. However, you and I can be life-giving in other ways. When we relieve someone's burden, bring freedom where it had been taken, proclaim the good news, or administer a kind word, we breathe life in God's name.

Grow Your Child's Faith

You can make someone feel alive and happy by using the breaths—and the life—God has given you. Maybe you could sing a song to make someone feel better or to celebrate how much you care. Maybe you could go to someone sad and say a nice thing that makes the tears stop.

Dear Father, thank You for all the breaths You've ever given me. Help me use the breaths You give me to help others feel alive and happy. Amen.

GOD SHOULD BE SERVED

We love because he first loved us.
1 John 4:19

Don't you love it when someone
does something nice for you?
Doesn't it make you want to
give that person a gift in return?

Like playing catch!
How can you throw a ball of giving
back to God?

Grow Your Faith

We often equate serving God only with ministry or volunteering
at church, but the ability to truly serve God is a lot bigger. What's
your favorite way to give back to God for all He's given you?

Grow Your Child's Faith

The Bible says that doing something nice for someone else—especially someone who is sad or hurting or sick or poor or unpopular—is a way to give a gift straight to God. What are five things God has done to make your life awesome? Now think of five things you can do for others to throw the ball back at God.

Dear Father, thank You for giving me so many good gifts. Show me how to thank You by doing something nice for someone else. Amen.

WE SHOULD WORSHIP GOD

"Worship the LORD your God."
2 Kings 17:39

Do you know what worship is?
When you love something so much
that you would give up everything for it,
you're worshipping that thing.

It's okay to love things and people,
but there's only one being
who should be worshipped
with all our hearts.

God.

Grow Your Faith

Many people worship the god known not as I AM but as "If Only." "If only I made more money …" "If only I was married …" "If only we had children …" Are there any "If Onlys" you're worshipping today?

Grow Your Child's Faith

There are many good reasons to worship God. First, God the Father designed the universe. Then, God the Father created all living things—that includes you. God the Father loves you and made a way for you to go to heaven when you die. That's so amazing!

Dear Father, You are the only One, the only being anywhere, who deserves my worship. Amen.

GOD CORRECTS US AS A FATHER SHOULD

"Blessed is the one whom God corrects."
Job 5:17

Sometimes I don't like it when someone tells me
I'm doing the wrong thing.
Do you?

God wants us to live in the right ways,
but sometimes we don't want to change
what we're doing.

Grow Your Faith

Nobody likes to receive correction. It's a notification we're doing the wrong thing, and maybe that's what we dislike most of all. Is there an area in your life you know God wants you to change? Consider making that change now.

Grow Your Child's Faith

Sometimes people—even grown-ups—get in trouble. They may feel bad for doing the wrong thing, but they also know life will be better if they learned how to not do wrong things. That's how it is when God wants to show us the right way to go. We wish we didn't get in trouble with Him, but we know we'll be better if we let Him do His loving work.

Dear Father, I don't like being told I'm doing wrong things. It makes me feel sad and sometimes angry. Please help me know that You give me consequences and even punishment not to hurt me but to help me live the way You know is best for me. Amen.

12

GOD LISTENS TO OUR PRAYERS

I call on you, my God, for you will answer me;
turn your ear to me and hear my prayer.

Psalm 17:6

Do you have someone you can tell anything to?
Someone who loves you so much
you can say what you really feel …
and not worry?

God's like that.

God always hears us.
God always listens.
God always answers,
but it may be yes, no, or wait.
Because God always loves us.

Grow Your Faith

Some people think God will cut them off if they sin one time too many. But the adoption papers He made out for you weren't written in disappearing ink. What would you tell God if you could tell Him anything and not worry?

Grow Your Child's Faith

We know God always hears us when we pray. Sometimes it seems like a one-way conversation, but God is always with us. The Bible can teach us to listen to Him, even when He speaks very quietly. That's why it's so important to get to know the Bible—so we can hear His answer.

Dear Father, thank You that You talk to me all the time. Please help me put lots of the Bible in my memory so You have more ways to tell me what You want me to hear. Amen.

THE HEAVENS DECLARE THE GLORY OF GOD

*The heavens declare the glory of God; the skies
proclaim the work of his hands.*

Psalm 19:1

The skies above us are like God's artwork,
hanging in a gallery over our heads.

When we see His art, we ought to take a minute
to tell the Artist how much we love it.

Grow Your Faith

The sun's diameter is 109 times larger than the Earth's. But that's tiny! The star VY Canis Majoris, a hypergiant 3,900 light years from earth, is 2,100 times larger than our own sun. That makes VY Canis Majoris 155,000 times larger than the Earth.[1]

Our God created the Earth, sun, and stars. Truly, the heavens declare the glory of God.

---

1   Jessica Orwig, "Crazy Image Shows How Tiny Earth Is
    Compared to Our Sun," *Business Insider*, January 13, 2015,
    www.businessinsider.com/earth-size-compared-to-sun-graphic-2015-1.

Grow Your Children's Faith

God didn't just create our world. He created all of space! And God is in control of everything He made. If God can put a comet way out at the other side of the universe and make it go where He wants, we can know He can also lead us.

Dear Father, thank You that You care a lot more about me—and all the other people in the world—than You do about comets and moons. You hold the universe together, and You love to hold me in Your lap. Thank You for caring for me! Amen.

14

GOD IS OUR REFUGE AND STRENGTH

God is our refuge and strength, an ever-present help in trouble.
Psalm 46:1

What do you want when a terrible storm comes along?
A safe place, right?

You want it to be strong against the wind.
You want it to be quiet against the thunderclaps.
You want it to be high against the floods.

That's what God is for you.

Grow Your Faith

Many of us try to handle life's storms on our own and sometimes find unhealthy ways to cope. How can you turn to God as your refuge and strength in times of trouble?

Grow Your Child's Faith

Can you think of a time when you felt scared and then something changed that made your fear disappear? What changed? How does God keep you safe?

Dear Father, I know that things won't always feel sunny and calm around me. I'm so glad You've put things in my life to take the fear away when it comes. Amen.

15

GOD SPEAKS WITH HIS SILENCE

"Be still, and know that I am God."
Psalm 46:10

Sometimes God's loudest shout
is a whisper,
and His biggest roar
is silence.

When we have to listen hard
and search for an answer,
we pay more attention
to what we find.

Grow Your Faith

Imagine you are deep in nature. Get far enough out that road noise and passing aircraft and sounds of the city are left behind. Then just listen. Listen with your eyes closed. Sometimes, God's voice is in the gentle breeze (see 1 Kings 19:11–13).

Grow Your Child's Faith

God the Father spoke to us through the Bible. He can speak in lots of other ways too, but He sometimes speaks very quietly. Can you hear God whispering? Practice being a good listener so you will hear God's quiet voice.

Dear Father, You're such a great keeper of secrets! I'm sending You my secret prayer, and I can't wait to get Your answer. Amen.

16

PRAISE GOD

Sing praises to God, sing praises; sing praises to our King, sing praises.
Psalm 47:6

Sometimes my heart is so full
of joy about God
that I can't keep it inside.
I have to sing!

Sing a loud song
to God about
how incredibly awesome
He is!

Grow Your Faith

Knowing God the Father can fill us with joy on a daily basis.

Grow Your Child's Faith

I dare you to make up the silliest, happiest song about God ever! Here's one: "God, You are so aw-aw-aw-aw-some I can't belee-lee-lee-leeve it! Soop-la-la, boomp-la-la. Belee-lee-leeve it! *Humph.*" Beat that!

Dear Father, You have known all the kids who have ever lived and are living and ever will live, and You love us all! That just makes me want to sing! Amen.

17

GOD LOVES A BROKEN SPIRIT

*The sacrifice you desire is a broken spirit. You will not
reject a broken and repentant heart, O God.*
Psalm 51:17 NLT

When you have "a broken spirit,"
it means you're humble.
It means you know
that sometimes you need forgiveness.

It means you know how much
you need God.

God loves anyone with a broken spirit.
He gives that person special love.
God moves nearer to the humble.

Grow Your Faith

Until we come to a place of humility, we can't receive all of what God wants to give. What areas of pride are holding you back?

Grow Your Child's Faith

When you see a whimpering puppy or a hurt baby bird, don't you want to just run to it to try to help? That's what it looks like to have a "broken spirit." God the Father loves to help anyone with a broken spirit.

Dear Father, please help me to always have a humble heart, because I know You love to fix what is broken. Amen.

18

OUR FATHER IN HEAVEN PERFORMS MIRACLES ON EARTH

You are the God who performs miracles.
Psalm 77:14

Have you ever seen a miracle?
Something that couldn't be explained
except by saying
God must've done it?

Or maybe just a private miracle
that God did only for you?
Just because He loves you
and knows you so well.

Grow Your Faith

How many miracles do we miss or explain away because we think God doesn't perform them anymore? How many broken fevers and non-fatal crashes are the direct intervention of God? Ask God to show you something you didn't realize He did, and then thank Him for it.

Grow Your Child's Faith

The same God who made everything from nothing, who created hippos and hummingbirds and the Himalayas, who invented day and night keeps His creation safe all the time. He works miracles that we don't understand and sometimes don't even notice. Thank God today for His miracles, even the ones you don't notice.

Dear Father, what miracle do You want me to see? Amen.

19

GOD'S LOVE ENDURES FOREVER

His love endures forever.
Psalm 136:2

Do you know someone who used to be your friend
and now you don't talk to anymore?

God's love doesn't change like ours does.
When God says He loves someone,
it's for keeps.
And God loves you.
Always.

Grow Your Faith

God warned us that many people's love would grow cold (see Matt. 24:12). We see that happening, don't we? But there are pockets of hope, warmth, and love—holdouts against hate. How can you be a conduit for God's eternal love today?

Grow Your Child's Faith

Some people—even kids—have been left behind or hurt. They don't know what real love is. How could you show someone that God's love for him or her is forever?

Dear Father, it's incredible to know Your love for me goes on forever and ever and You don't change Your mind about me. Could You please give me a chance to tell someone about Your forever love? Amen.

20

GOD'S WORD IS PERFECT

"Every word of God is flawless."
Proverbs 30:5

Do you ever wish life came
with a map?

It does, actually.

The Bible is God's
perfect book of directions
for how to live.

Grow Your Faith

Think about the situations you're facing right now. Is there a Bible principle you haven't tried yet that you could try in that situation?

Grow Your Child's Faith

When you can't figure out why you are lost and confused, read God's map. Psalm 119 celebrates God's words because they shed light on how to live. Look up Psalm 119:105 in the Bible and read it out loud.

Dear Father, thank You for the Bible. Teach me how to read it so I can learn all the things You want me to know so I can live in the ways You like. Amen.

21

GOD COMFORTS HIS PEOPLE

"Comfort, comfort my people," says your God.
Isaiah 40:1 NLT

Is there anything better
than a giant hug?

Especially one that makes you feel safe
and promises that everything
is going to be all right.

And one day
God will hug you
with His own arms.

Grow Your Faith

God comforts us so we can do the same for others (see 2 Cor. 1:4).
It almost seems like He gives us some of that comfort so we can
give it away to someone else. Who could you comfort today?

Grow Your Child's Faith

Sometimes we're hurting, and God hugs us through someone else.
It helps, doesn't it? Other times, someone else is hurting. When

you give kindness to someone who is sad, you are being like God the Father.

Dear Father, one way I think of You is always standing there with Your arms open so I can run up and get a big hug from You whenever I want it. Help me give Your hugs to other people too. Amen.

22

GOD WILL GIVE MERCY AND PARDON TO US

Let the wicked ... and the unrighteous ... turn to the LORD, and he
will have mercy on them, and to our God, for he will freely pardon.
Isaiah 55:7

When two people are play-wrestling,
sometimes the one who is pinned
will yell, "Mercy!"
It means, "I give up! You win!"

Pardon is when a judge could punish us
but decides to let us go instead.

All of us do things that God could punish us for.
But He would much rather have mercy and give pardon.
He's only waiting for us to ask.

Grow Your Faith

Are you withholding mercy or pardon from anyone? Consider granting it today. You'll be set free!

Grow Your Child's Faith

God likes it when His kids act like He acts. We can't create a universe like He did, but we can copy Him in other ways. Like forgiving people who are mean to us or hurt us. Is there anyone you want to keep hurting because of what he or she did to you? Today, what if you were to be like God and forgive that person forever?

Dear Father, it's so hard to forgive people who hurt me. But I don't like how bad I feel when I hang on to my anger. Please help me forgive them. Thank You for how You've forgiven me! Amen.

23

GOD'S WORD SUSTAINS OUR SOULS

"No one can live only on food. People need
every word that God has spoken."
Matthew 4:4 CEV

Without food, your body would die.
But the thing that keeps our hearts and souls alive
is the Bible—the words of God the Father.

Have you "eaten" some of it today?
Why not have a huge feast of it?

Grow Your Faith

Reading the Bible is a great way to keep yourself joined to the vine
(see John 15:1–5). If you haven't had your helping today, why not
read all of John 15? It'll do your body good!

Grow Your Child's Faith

What would it be like to eat at a king's table? The food would taste amazing and be served in fancy dishes, and there'd probably be tons of it. That's what reading the Bible is like! God, our King, made a feast that would feed our hearts and souls, and we "eat" it by reading the Bible. For today's meal, let's read the story of what happened to a boy named Samuel (see 1 Sam. 3).

Dear Father, You know how to keep my body strong with food, and it's so cool that You gave me something to keep my soul strong too! Please give me a love for reading the Bible—the words of You, my King! Amen.

24

GOD PROVIDES DAILY FOR US

"Give us today our daily bread."
Matthew 6:11

Your heavenly Father promises
to give you
what you need each day.

Today, God gives you the love and comfort
you need for today,
not all the love and comfort
you'll need for the rest of your life.

God gives you what you need
one day at a time.
Right on time.

Grow Your Faith

Many of us wish we could have money for tomorrow—all our tomorrows—today. For many of us, God doesn't work like that. He delights in having us help each other as we can.

Grow Your Child's Faith

What's going to happen tomorrow? You think you know at least some of it, but you could be totally wrong. God the Father *does* know, and He's got you covered.

Dear Father, thank You that You hold all my days and know all the things that are going to happen to me. Thank You for knowing exactly what I need! Amen.

25

GOD FORGIVES AS WE FORGIVE

"Forgive us for doing wrong, as we forgive others."
Matthew 6:12 CEV

Jesus taught that God the Father
forgives us in the same way
we forgive people around us.

That kind of scares me,
because sometimes I don't want to forgive.

But if God is going to forgive me—or not—
in the same way I forgive other people …
I want to forgive!

Grow Your Faith

Has a person really tasted of God's mercy if he or she is wishing for someone else to suffer? The hallmark of God's love upon us is that it makes us eager—even desperate—to get out and give that love to others so they too can be set free.

Grow Your Child's Faith

When we forgive people who are mean to us, we're acting like God, who loves to forgive. Is there anyone you need to forgive right now?

Dear Father, sometimes people really hurt my feelings. Sometimes I don't want to forgive them. Help me be willing to forgive people, even if they don't really seem sorry. You're a forgiving God, and I want to be like You. Amen.

26

WE CANNOT SERVE GOD AND MONEY

"No one can serve two masters. Either you will hate the one and love the other, or you will be devoted to the one and despise the other. You cannot serve both God and money."
Matthew 6:24

Money can seem almost like God.
With enough money,
you can do almost anything.

But money's power has limits.
It can't create a galaxy.
It can't hear your prayers.
And it definitely can't
take you to heaven when you die.

Grow Your Faith

It's not a sin for Christians to be wealthy. But riches can easily become idols, whether or not you have them. How can you use your money to worship God instead of worshipping money itself?

Grow Your Child's Faith

God cares about you. Sometimes people think that God loves rich or poor people more, but He loves everyone the same. How can you use money to show God you love Him too?

Dear Father, it does seem that life is easier when we have money. But if I ever have to choose between having You and money, help me to always choose You! Amen.

27

GOD PROVIDES FOR GRASS AND BIRDS ... AND YOU

"Look at the birds ... your heavenly Father feeds
them.... If that is how God clothes the grass of the
field, which is here today and tomorrow is thrown into
the fire, will he not much more clothe you ..."
Matthew 6:26, 30

Do birds fly to work every morning
to earn their food?
Does the grass wander over to the store
to pick out some nice new clothes?

That's crazy!
God gives them everything they need.
If God watches over birds and grass,
you can be sure He watches over you too.

Grow Your Faith

Some people worry about having what they need, no matter how much they have! God's people are told not to worry. God loves you and takes care of you in all circumstances. What will your child see when you stop worrying and start trusting God to provide?

Grow Your Child's Faith

Birds fly through the air and find the food God has given them. The grass seeks the sun and grows healthy. The birds and the grass don't worry about whether or not they'll have what they need, and we shouldn't either. No matter how much or how little we have, God still has us in His arms.

Dear Father, thank You that You love me even more than the amazing world of plants and animals You have made. Thank You that You watch over me and care for me every day, at every meal, and every time I get dressed. I'm so glad You love me! Amen.

28

GOD LOVES TO GIVE GIFTS

*"So if you sinful people know how to give good gifts
to your children, how much more will your heavenly
Father give good gifts to those who ask him."*
Matthew 7:11 NLT

God the Father's heart
is like a human father's heart,
except God's heart is much bigger
and more generous.

If a father's generosity is an inch,
God the Father's generosity is a million miles.

Grow Your Faith

God has His eyes on targets different from the ones we tend to focus on. We want to be comfortable; He wants us to be holy. We want gifts that help us now; He gives us gifts for our eternal good. He wants us to have treasure in heaven even more than treasure on earth.

Grow Your Child's Faith

God the Father is a big believer in showering His children with joy, life, and fun. Human fathers do the best they can, but nobody can out-give God!

Dear Father, thank You that You're the best father ever. Thank You that You think it's fun to give gifts! Amen.

29

GOD WANTS ALL OF US TO LIVE FOREVER WITH HIM

"Your Father in heaven is not willing that any of these little ones should perish."
Matthew 18:14

While we're here on earth,
we make choices.
And when the time is up,
there's no more choosing.

Some of our choices are tiny,
but some of them are huge.
And there's one choice that is the biggest ever.

God wants every person in the world
to choose Him
and to live with Him forever in heaven.

Grow Your Faith

No matter your age, you're one of God's little ones. God desperately desires you to be with Him in the new heaven and new earth that will come after this one. Have you given your heart to Him? If not, the invitation stands open.

Grow Your Child's Faith

There are only two forever places to choose between. One is good, and it's called heaven. People who choose heaven will live forever with God, having fun, exploring, doing cool work, and hanging around with God the Father and the angels. Choose heaven!

Dear Father, I don't fully understand what heaven will be like. But I love You and know that You're good. When I'm ready, would You please help me make my choice to be with You? Amen.

30

GOD CAN DO ANYTHING

"With God all things are possible."
Matthew 19:26

God can do anything
and everything.
Is there something
He can't do?
Absolutely not!

Grow Your Faith

Even though we know, in theory, that God can do anything, sometimes we think He really can't. Just for fun, take something that seems impossible to you—something of intense value to you—and ask our impossibly powerful God, one more time, to do it.

Grow Your Child's Faith

God can do anything, but He doesn't alwasy do what we ask. That can be hard to understand. We can believe He's doing what's best for us all the time.

Dear Father, it's incredible that You can do anything. It must be strange and wonderful to have as much power as You do. Thank You that You use it all so well! Amen.

31

LOVE GOD COMPLETELY

*"Love the Lord your God with all your heart and
with all your soul and with all your mind."*

Matthew 22:37

What if a bride and groom
stood in a church on their wedding day,
and the bride said,
"I will give you only half my heart"?

God never gives only half His heart.
And He asks us to love Him
with our whole hearts too.

Grow Your Faith

Loving God fully isn't a *condition* of our salvation. It is a *result* of it. What's the natural reaction to someone who gives and gives to us? When we're confronted with wholehearted devotion, all we want to do is give it right back.

Grow Your Child's Faith

Is there someone who loves to give you gifts? When that person thinks about you, he or she just gets crazy happy and wants to give you more and more. God loves you with that kind of crazy love, and as you grow, your love for God will grow too.

Dear Father, it's so fantastic that You—the God of the universe—love me like I'm Your favorite! It's like a party whenever we think about each other. I want my love for You to grow so it's as big as Your love for me. Amen.

32

GOD ALONE KNOWS JESUS' RETURN

"No one knows the day or hour. The angels in heaven don't know, and the Son himself doesn't know. Only the Father knows."
Matthew 24:36 CEV

Did you know that there is one secret
that is so secret
only God the Father knows?

Even Jesus doesn't know!

The one secret God keeps
from *everyone* else
is the year, month, day, hour, minute, and second
Jesus will come back to earth.

Grow Your Faith

Why do you think God withholds the timing of Jesus' return from everyone, even Jesus? This question reminds us that although we can know God and a lot about Him, God is mysterious. We do not know His specific plans, but we can trust that they are good.

Grow Your Child's Faith

God the Father has only one secret He's kept from everyone else. What if He's doing that so He can come to Jesus and the Holy Spirit and all the angels one morning and say, "Wake up, everybody. Today's the day! Jesus is going back to earth today, and our forever party is beginning right now!" Can you imagine the cheering and celebrating there would be in heaven that day?

Dear Father, You give good gifts and shower people with love. Thank You for loving us so much that You gave us Jesus and are sending Him to earth again. Amen.

33

GOD COULD SEND THOUSANDS OF ANGELS

"Do you think I cannot call on my Father, and he will at once put at my disposal more than twelve legions of angels?"
Matthew 26:53

When Jesus was on the cross,
whole armies of angels could've
come to His rescue
if He'd called for them.

Maybe the thing that made God most proud
was that Jesus *didn't* call for the angel armies.
Jesus chose to stay on the cross and not be rescued
so we could be rescued instead
and go to heaven when we die.

Grow Your Faith

How hard is it to let our children go through terrible pain? Everything in us wants to make it stop—or to take their place. God let His Son suffer so that many more sons and daughters could live with Him. How great is the Father's love for us!

Grow Your Child's Faith

Jesus chose to die on the cross to take our punishment for us. God the Father could have sent mighty angels to save Jesus, but they agreed on their plan and stuck to it. How hard it must have been to be so powerful and not take action!

Dear Father, I can't imagine how hard it must've been for You to watch Jesus die. It must've been terrible for You to not send those angels to save Jesus. But thank You for what came out of all that pain. Amen.

34

FORGIVE EACH OTHER ON THE WAY

"If your enemy is taking you to court, become friends quickly, before you go to court. Otherwise, your enemy might turn you over to the judge."

Matthew 5:25 NCV

Once there were two kids who had an argument at school.
They got in trouble and were sent to the office.
This principal liked to give big consequences
unless the kids had made up on their own.

While they were waiting to see him,
they talked it out and said they were sorry.

The principal heard them and smiled.
They'd worked it out!
So he sent them to recess,
and all of them had a good day.

Grow Your Faith

Isn't life too short to hold grudges? What we see throughout history is God the Father making a way for us to be reconciled. Consider making the decision to be reconciled with anyone you may be holding onto bitterness about.

Grow Your Child's Faith

Our lives are kind of like a bus ride to somewhere far away. We don't know how long it will last. All we do know is that, when the ride is over, we won't have any more chances to make things right with people we got mad at. Is there someone you need to talk with to heal your friendship?

Dear Father, thank You that You give us this lifetime to make friends and even to make things right with people. Please make me brave enough to at least try to fix things with the people I've been mad at or hurt by. Amen.

35

GOD GAVE HIS SON FOR YOU

"For God so loved the world that he gave his one and only Son, that whoever believes in him shall not perish but have eternal life."
John 3:16

What would you be willing to give up
to save your pet?
What would you be willing to give up
to save your mom or dad?

There are some things
we care about so much
that we'd be willing
to give anything to save them.

God gave the life of
His own Son for you.
What does that say about how much
He loves you?

Grow Your Faith

It's fascinating to think about God's decision to sacrifice His Son in order to save humankind. God knew the resurrection was a nonnegotiable part of the plan. He knew He'd get all of humankind *and* His Son back in the bargain. Still, it was painful to go through. Only love kept Jesus on the cross.

Grow Your Child's Faith

Is there someone in your life who you would gladly give away every one of your toys to help? You'd have to love that person with all your heart to give like that. God didn't give away a toy; He offered His precious Son. How amazing is God's love!

Dear Father, I can't even imagine giving up my family to save someone else. Thank You for loving us so much You gave up Your Son for us. Amen.

36

GOD THE FATHER WORKS

"My Father is always working, and so am I."
John 5:17 NLT

God is always up to something incredible.
He created the universe in six days,
took only one day off,
and then went back to work.
All because He loves His creation.

You and I can look around—
any day and every day—
and *always* spot someone
who needs some loving.

Grow Your Faith

Jobs provide special opportunities for Christians. A job is one place we come into contact with the same people over and over again—people who desperately need the love of God. It's pretty cool to get paid to love people in God's name!

Grow Your Child's Faith

God loves to give people all around the world the chance to get to know Him. You can help God if you tell someone else about Him. Be looking around every day for people you can love in the way God would love them.

Dear Father, You're always working! You're always painting sunrises and healing broken hearts and calling people to You. Help me be a worker like You. Please let me be part of the great work You're doing! Amen.

37

OUR FATHER'S HOME HAS A SPECIAL PLACE FOR US

*"My Father's house has many rooms ... I am
going there to prepare a place for you."*
John 14:2

When Jesus was about to leave the earth,
He said He was going to get a place ready for us
in God the Father's great house.

What will your room look like?
Will we really be living in a house at all?
All we know for sure is that God and Jesus will be there,
and there's plenty of room for all of us who believe in them.

Grow Your Faith

If you could design heaven, what would it be like? Would everyone sit around on clouds strumming harps? Would we all get to play our favorite sports? Would we spend a billion years at a time having worship services around God's throne? What would you create?

Grow Your Child's Faith

One day, on the day only God the Father knows, everything will be ready, and Jesus will come back to earth to get all of us who love Him. We'll go be with Him forever in the heavenly place He's built for us. Pretty awesome, huh?

Dear Father, I don't know what heaven is going to be like, but from what I know about You, I bet there will be a lot of joy. Thank You! Amen.

38

GROW FRUIT FOR GOD THE FATHER

"This is to my Father's glory, that you bear much fruit."
John 15:8

The good and loving things we do
because we are God's children
are like wonderful, juicy fruit
that show people we belong to God.

God wants us to do those things—
to bear that tasty fruit—
so others will come to Him
and become His children too.

Grow Your Faith

Waht would happen if God took us to heaven the moment we committed our lives to Him? No one would be left to share the good news! If getting saved yourself was the only purpose of this life, then life would have ended at the moment you believed. But God wants people of faith to draw others to Him—others who are not yet His.

Grow Your Child's Faith

Have you ever seen something so amazing you had to stop and take a closer look? That's how we're supposed to be as children of God. We're supposed to act in good and loving ways that show we are connected to God. Then people will want to stop and take a closer look. What's something you could do for someone that would make him or her want to know more about God?

Dear Father, help me produce good fruit so people will want to come closer and learn about You. Amen.

39

OBEY GOD THE FATHER

"We don't obey people. We obey God."
Acts 5:29 CEV

We should obey our teachers, the principal,
police and firefighters, doctors,
and our parents.

But what if the people in charge
told you to stop loving God?
Who would you obey?

Grow Your Faith

Many of us will never have to face real persecution. But we can face other kinds of resistance. It can be a disapproving look or a mumbled comment. It can be a shove or vandalism or a promotion going to someone else. Consider making this your plan: "Make up your mind not to worry beforehand how you will defend yourselves. For I will give you words and wisdom that none of your adversaries will be able to resist or contradict" (Luke 21:14–15).

Grow Your Child's Faith

Did you know that some kids in the world have to decide between loving God and obeying someone in charge? Let's pray for them right now and ask God to protect them.

Dear Father, I want to obey You no matter what happens. Please help me be brave and remember that even if I mess up, You will always love me. Amen.

40

GOD DOES EXTRAORDINARY MIRACLES

God did extraordinary miracles though Paul.
Acts 19:11

What is a miracle?
When a woman who can't walk can suddenly run?
When a blind man can suddenly see?
When someone survives a terrible car crash?

God performed so many miracles.
From creating *everything*
to keeping His eye on you and me,
God is a miracle-working God.

Grow Your Faith

One of the most powerful miracles in our world is a life transformed by God. The child of God, walking in full awareness of his or her forgiveness, is a channel of God's love into the world. And wherever God's love is channeled, miracles happen.

Grow Your Child's Faith

Sometimes we think it would be easier to follow God if miracles happened more often. Who wouldn't love a God who did extraordinary things all the time? But God wants people to love Him even when He's not doing miracles.

Dear Father, thank You that You have the power to do miracles. Thank You that You can always make one happen anytime You want. Amen.

41

WE MUST HONOR GOD WITH OUR BODIES

God paid a great price for you. So use your body to honor God.
1 Corinthians 6:20 CEV

What if someone bought something for a million dollars
and asked you to take care of it?
Would you throw it down the stairs
or toss it in a lake?

God gave you your body.
Did you know that?
And Jesus paid for your soul.
Take good care of your body.

Grow Your Faith

Are you honoring God by how you treat your body? Consider if there's anything you could change today that would help you be able to honor God more as you parent your child, spend time with your family, or go to work.

Grow Your Child's Faith

God wants us all to take care of our bodies. Burgers and cake are great, but water and exercise and healthy food are very important too. This is the only body you get on earth. Take care of it now and every day, and you'll be ready to do the amazing things God has planned for you.

Dear Father, thank You for all the things my body can do. Help me take good care of it and use it to bring joy to You. Amen.

42

GOD CREATES ORDER AND PEACE

God is not a God of confusion but a God of peace.
1 Corinthians 14:33 NCV

Sometimes, even when we follow God,
life can seem confusing.
But the next time you feel like that,
just relax.
God is the inventor of how to put things in order.

If you were given all the parts of a car,
it might look like a puzzling pile of junk.
But a master mechanic knows just where everything goes.

Grow Your Faith

One of the greatest Christian challenges is to see only one part of the picture and yet somehow walk in the perfect confidence that everything is going according to a master plan.

Grow Your Child's Faith

The next time life confused you, think of God standing like a mechanic surrounded by the parts of a car. Imagine Him whistling happily as He expertly picks out one thing and fits it into another thing, just as calm and peaceful as He can be. That's what God is like in the universe, and it's what God is like in your life.

Dear Father, it's hard to be human sometimes. When I'm confused and afraid, please help me remember You're in charge of it all! Amen.

43

GOD GIVES US VICTORY

But we thank God! He gives us the victory
through our Lord Jesus Christ.
1 Corinthians 15:57 NCV

It's great to be on the winning team.

Spoiler alert!

At the end of the Bible,
God's team wins.

Grow Your Faith

When we read social media or watch the news, it sounds like the world is in a crisis of, well, biblical proportions. It can leave us fearful, angry, or discouraged. It's helpful to remember that God made this universe and is actually moving things toward the destination He had in mind from the beginning.

Grow Your Child's Faith

Bad things sometimes happen. But one day we will be in a place where there are no more tears, no more disease, and no more pain. It's called heaven, and we get to be there forever with God the Father, who made it all in the first place.

Dear Father, I'm glad I'm on Your team. It will be so amazing to be with You forever in the place where we celebrate Your victory! Amen.

44

GOD IS JUST

God is just.
2 Thessalonians 1:6

Have you ever heard someone say,
"That's not fair"?
Have you ever said that?

Sometimes when we say something isn't fair,
we mean we didn't get a good thing
someone else got.

Guess what? God isn't fair.
But He is just.
And that's much better.

Grow Your Faith

When we come to maturity in God, we understand there is no need for us to get what's fair. We're complete in Him even if we don't get the same thing the next person gets. How much better would it be to work to help others be treated justly than to worry about what we didn't receive? Today, be a champion for justice.

Grow Your Child's Faith

Fairness is when everyone gets the same amount of the same thing. But justice is better. Justice means that people should be treated well, but when they're not something is done to make it right. The world will never be fair. But as a child of God the Father, what's one thing you could do to make it more just?

Dear Father, I'm sorry that sometimes I get upset when someone else gets more than I do. Help me not to worry about what's fair and help me start caring about helping other people. Amen.

45

GOD BREATHED HIS WORD FOR US

All Scripture is God-breathed.
2 Timothy 3:16

Every word of Scripture
is "God-breathed."
God breathed it.

God breathed out the words,
"Let there be light,"
and there was light.
Jesus is called the Word of God.

The Bible you hold in your hand
is the very breath of heaven.

Grow Your Faith

Most Christians tend to focus on their favorite parts of the Bible, but they may miss out on important teachings. Be brave. Go exploring. *All* Scripture is God-breathed. All of it is useful vocabulary God will use to tell you what He wants you to do.

Grow Your Child's Faith

Some parts of the Bible are harder to understand than other parts. But all of it is important and teaches us something about God. If you're reading a verse you don't understand, ask someone to explain it. If no one can make it make sense to you, don't worry! It'll still be there when you're older and know more about God for yourself.

Dear Father, thank You that we have Your voice, Your words, and Your breath right in our Bibles! Help me to understand it more. Amen.

46

GOD IS THE STOREHOUSE OF WISDOM

*If any of you lacks wisdom, you should ask
God, who gives generously to all.*

James 1:5

Have you ever heard of wisdom?
Remember the wise men
who brought gold, frankincense, and myrrh
to baby Jesus?

Wisdom isn't knowing a lot.
Wisdom isn't being smart.
Wisdom isn't remembering information.

Wisdom is the understanding God gives
of what things really mean
and what to do about them.

Grow Your Faith

Wisdom comes through living, hurting, and making mistakes. You've lived long enough to have acquired some wisdom. Some of it came through your insights and experiences you never asked for. What's a wonderful word of wisdom you could pass on to your child today?

Grow Your Child's Faith

Sometimes we gain wisdom by going through pain, like learning not to touch the hot stove. But sometimes we gain wisdom just by asking God for it. God can help us understand things that would never make sense otherwise. And He can help us be okay with not understanding some things too.

Dear Father, would You give me wisdom and make me like You? Amen.

47

GOD CANNOT BE TEMPTED

*God cannot be tempted by evil, and he
doesn't use evil to tempt others.*
James 1:13 CEV

Have you ever really, really wanted
something you shouldn't have?
Like when there's a special dessert
being saved for a celebration,
and you walk by it just to look at it again?

That's temptation: when you want something
you know you're not supposed to have.

Grow Your Faith

Sometimes when Christians encounter opportunities to sin, they
tell themselves it means God must be encouraging them to sin.
"Encouragement to sin" is a good definition of *temptation*. It's not
something God will ever do. Encouragement to sin comes from
our own desires, the false stories we tell ourselves, and the Devil,
but *never* from God.

Grow Your Child's Faith

Sometimes you really, really want to do a thing you're not supposed to. Remember that God wasn't the one pushing you to do the wrong thing. What can you do to resist doing something bad?

Dear Father, I wish I always did the thing You want me to do, but I know I don't. And I'll probably do the wrong things a lot in my life. I know You don't want me to do wrong. Please help me get stronger at choosing the right thing. Amen.

48

GOD IS LIGHT

God is light; in him there is no darkness at all.
1 John 1:5

You can see one candle in a dark room.
It's not even hard!

Our world can be dark
because of bad things people do.
But that makes it even easier
to see how different and good God is.

Grow Your Faith

Our purest idea of light is the sun. The sun is a giant ball of raging power—purifying heat and penetrating light with no possibility of shadow. That's the sort of light God is. The closer we get to Him in our hearts, the fewer shadows we can—or want to—hide in. We welcome His searching, cleansing, exposing presence because we are secure in His love and want to yield to His design.

Grow Your Child's Faith

Light helps us feel safe—especially at night. Light helps us see that everything is okay. That we're okay. So when you hear that God is light, how does that make you feel? There's no darkness in Him at all. Isn't that amazing?

Dear Father, it's so cool that You are light and love me, protect me, and watch over me. Thank You! Amen.

49

GOD IS LOVE

God is love.
1 John 4:8

God doesn't just have love,
He *is* love.
And what He is,
He does.

God loves you,
and God loves me.
Because He loved us first,
we love Him.

Grow Your Faith

Sometimes people are so identified with a quality or activity that they come to represent it. Like saying, "This one teacher wasn't just a good part of that school for me, she *was* that school for me." God is love, so what's one way you can express that love to someone today?

Grow Your Child's Faith

God is love. That means everything He does is loving. If someone is mean to Him, His answer is love. If someone is lonely, His answer is love. If someone makes a terrible choice, His answer is love. If you ever worry you've made God mad, remember He is love, and His answer to you is always going to come from what He is.

Dear Father, the idea that You are love is the most amazing and important thing I have ever learned. Show me how to live like I know You are love. Amen.

50

WE CANNOT
SEE GOD WITH
HUMAN EYES

No one has ever seen God.

1 John 4:12

God is invisible.
He is spirit and light and love.
He's in all places at all times.

One of the reasons Jesus came to earth
was so people could see
what God is like.
Whoever saw Jesus saw God the Father.

Jesus only ever did
what He saw His Father doing.

Grow Your Faith

God told Moses no one could survive seeing the face of God (see Ex. 33:20). One day, we'll get new bodies that can endure the pure holiness of God. In the meantime, we can invite His holy presence into our hearts and lives in ever-increasing measure.

Grow Your Child's Faith

Sometimes it's hard to love a God we can't see. But think of it like loving people you know but don't live near. Those people are there and your love for them is huge even though you can't see them in real life today.

Dear Father, I wish I could see You. But I'm so glad You're everywhere so I'm never really alone. Amen.

51

GOD WIPES AWAY OUR TEARS

"God will wipe away every tear from their eyes."
Revelation 7:17

In heaven, our last tear
will be wiped away,
and all sadness
will be wiped away with it.

Grow Your Faith

When we think about the sorrow and tears that will be abolished in heaven, we're thinking about our own sorrow and tears. But consider that God has had more than His share of sorrow too. God is also excited for the day when we live with Him in heaven, when *none* of us will be sad again.

Grow Your Child's Faith

The people who love you do all they can to help you when you're hurting, sad, or afraid. Imagine what it will be like when God the Father kneels down and wipes away the very last tear you will ever have.

Dear Father, sometimes this life is really hard. Sometimes I hurt. I like my life, this world, and my family and friends, but I am so excited to get to heaven and be with You forever! Amen.

52

THE GLORY OF GOD IS THE LIGHT OF HEAVEN

It shone with the glory of God.
Revelation 21:11

The glory of God
is the light of heaven.

The glory of God
never gets dim,
never stops,
and never even sleeps.

It is forever.
How glorious is that?

Grow Your Faith

Paul wrote, "For now we see only a reflection as in a mirror; then we shall see face to face. Now I know in part; then I shall know fully, even as I am fully known" (1 Cor. 13:12). Paul's words are even more significant when we realize that ancient mirrors were made of polished metal, and the images they reflected weren't very clear at all. Paul was saying that we've only caught a glimpse of true glory. What do you look forward to most about seeing Jesus face-to-face?

Grow Your Child's Faith

Sometimes we have so much fun playing outside that we don't even notice when it gets dark. How awesome would it be for bright lights to turn on so we could keep playing as long as we want? In heaven, God's party will be so fun we'll never want it to stop. And because God is light and that light will shine forever, the party never has to stop.

Dear Father, just having You in my life makes me feel so happy, safe, and loved. I can't imagine how incredible it will be to be with You all the time. I can't wait! Amen.